First Time Dads Pregnancy Handbook

All You Need to Know to Survive and Thrive - Week by Week Pregnancy Development, What to Expect and How to Prepare

Ralph Smith

losses, direct or indirect, that are incurred as a result of the use of the information contained within this document, including, but not limited to, errors, omissions, or inaccuracies.

Table of Contents

INTRODUCTION...1

CHAPTER 1: PREGNANCY DEVELOPMENT 3

CHAPTER 2: BUILDING A HEALTHY RELATIONSHIP WITH THE
MOTHER OF YOUR UNBORN CHILD 25

CHAPTER 3: CONNECTING WITH YOUR UNBORN CHILD 33

CHAPTER 4: BIRTHING PLANS 39

CHAPTER 5: THE ARRIVAL OF THE BABY 47

CONCLUSION...59

REFERENCES...63

Introduction

Pregnancy at any stage of life is a new and exciting experience, and it can be a stressful and fearful time, especially when it is your first time going through a pregnancy experience. Hence, raising your awareness of what to expect during pregnancy and having a good support structure is vital during this life-changing time. Becoming your ideal parent as a first-time dad will require you to put your time and energy into the experience and become a provider, nurturer, protector, and empathetic and caring towards your child and the mother of your child. From learning the basics of the stages of pregnancy, and connecting with an unborn child, to tips on self-care and different parenting styles, the *First-Time Dads Pregnancy Handbook* provides all the information you need to survive and thrive - week by week pregnancy development, what to expect, and how to prepare!

It includes questions to ask yourself with the healthcare professional on how you want your delivery to be like, reflective questions on fatherhood, and more information. This realistic, friendly, to-the-point and informative pregnancy book will also share relatable stories from other first-time dads to inspire and empower. Find solace and peace of mind with this light-hearted first-time dad's pregnancy book. It will educate you on everything you need to know to become your ideal parent.

Chapter 1:

Pregnancy Development

In the pregnancy process I have come to realize how much of the burden is on the female partner. She's got a construction zone going on in her belly. —Al Roker

Pregnancy as a father-to-be will not equate to the experience of the mother-to-be, but it is a joint baby-growing adventure. You, as the father-to-be, may not be experiencing pregnancy symptoms, such as fatigue, frequent urination, morning 'til night sickness, aching back and feet, nausea, bloating, and the list goes on of the many pregnancy symptoms mothers-to-be come to experience. But you know what? As the father-to-be, you can certainly provide support and reassurance to her and your unborn child as the pregnancy progresses that you are there for them. Your role during this time is monumental, and here is what you can expect week by week of the stages of pregnancy and tips to help you along the way.

Week one and two - During this stage, there is no fetus in the womb just yet. Your partner is experiencing ovulation, whereby one of her eggs breaks out of one of her ovaries and moves down the fallopian tube to her uterus. The uterus is where your child will grow and receive nurturing for the next nine months of its life. However, before it gets to the uterus, the egg will move towards the sperm to begin the fertilization process. The fertilization process is beyond beautiful, and some would say it is miraculous how the female body can turn a fertilized egg into a child (Rodgers, 2020).

Week three - By this time, the sperm would have met with the egg and merged into a single cell that will grow steadily, and then nine to ten months later, a baby will be conceived, and then your life will never be the same again in a positive way, of course. Both of you may not know the biological and scientific cell division that occurs after fertilization, so take your mind off it for a short while and allow nature to take its course. Grab your favorite snack and binge-watch that series you want to stream to get your mind off the pregnancy development for a bit (Rodgers, 2020).

Week four - You may want to wait before buying a home pregnancy test at this time or making a doctor's appointment to get confirmation of the pregnancy - it is a week too early for that. While you are probably thinking about this and when the test results come out positive in a week or so, this would be a great time to think about the habits that both of you have as soon-to-be parents that will be harmful to your unborn baby (Rodgers, 2020). For example, if you are a smoker or both of you are smokers, then first-hand or second-hand smoking is dangerous for the baby's development as it may cause health complications or medical conditions. These include cleft lip or palate, low birth weight, and even sudden infant death syndrome (Centers for Disease Control and Prevention, 2022). Think about changing such unhealthy and dangerous habits for your mother-to-be and unborn child to have a good pregnancy. You could even start taking brisk walks in the morning with the mother of your unborn child. Perhaps, you could take brisk walks after breakfast four times a week. It will help reduce the risk of having a Cesarean section birth, backaches, shortened labor, bloating, swelling, and it will improve mood and energy levels, muscle tone, strength, endurance, and more (Mayo Clinic, 2022). Hopefully, taking on these healthy habits will help both of you to feel better than ever and be in good shape for the entire pregnancy (Rodgers, 2020).

Week five - By this time, it would be a great time to get that home pregnancy test and take it. The result will be positive! Congratulations are in order! Your unborn child would be the same length, width, and weight as an orange seed, and your mother-to-be will be showing early signs of pregnancy, such as aches and pains, tender breasts, fatigue, and nausea (Rodgers, 2020). You might want to take up more chores around the house so that she does not strain herself or accidentally harm your unborn child by lifting certain things. If you have pet cats, please do not let your partner clean the cat litter boxes because their feces are known to contain parasites that can carry a disease called toxoplasmosis. They can pass it on to unsuspecting hosts when they happen to come into contact with infected feces, especially when cleaning litter boxes infested with this disease. Even though it is a rare disease, it can be harmful to the unborn child.

Week six - Typically, nausea will begin to plague the mother-to-be. The commonly used term "morning sickness" is not entirely accurate in that expectant mothers only get sick in the morning. Mothers-to-be can experience nausea in the morning, afternoon, and night (Rodgers, 2020). Unfortunately, if they have not eaten anything that can increase nausea, you can give her healthy snacks, such as dried fruits, trail mix, unsalted nuts and raisins, granola bars, and roasted chickpeas (Clarke, 2022). These healthy snacks can be stored in a cupboard near her bed on a nightstand to take small bites when she gets up in the morning. If your partner finds it difficult to eat full meals, it would be beneficial to keep already made snacks and foods, such as whole grains and complex carbohydrates. Or, perhaps you could whip up smoothies, which are easy and quick to make and light on the stomach (Rodgers, 2020).

Week seven - You might find that the mother of your unborn child has an extremely good sense of smell that is probably 1,000 times stronger than a dog. That means, typically, she can smell any odor that piques her nostrils, whether it is the smell of a sweet and fresh orange fruit from afar or an offensive odor close to her. She could even propel herself to run towards that smell that has piqued her sense of smell or move away from it, even if it may lead her to escape an offensive odor, such as smelly socks and shoes, by going to the next room. You might unexpectedly need to let go of your cologne or put your socks and shoes away if she says they smell bad. And do it without feeling hurt or resentful because she is carrying your child and going through a transformational period (Rodgers, 2020).

Week eight - By these days of the pregnancy, the mother of your child might be experiencing lots more food aversions than usual. Whatever foods she cannot stomach, ensure to choose foods that are good for both the baby and the mother and satisfies her cravings (Rodgers, 2020).

Week nine - Her mammary glands or breasts will be fuller than before, but please be mindful of the fact that they will feel immensely tender to her. You will need to be very gentle and go easy during sexual intercourse because any sensations around her breasts and nipples might be too much during this time, even if it is the most delicate or slightest touch (Rodgers, 2020).

Week ten - By this time, she will regularly have doctor appointments for prenatal checkups, and she will continue attending doctor appointments until the day she gives birth. If you have a busy schedule, make time to go with her to these appointments, and if you are not allowed to be in the doctor's room with her due to restrictions, do ask whether you can video call during the appointment. It would be a wonderful gesture of love as long as you can be there, whether virtually or in person, to show your moral support to the two most important people in your life. Remember to ask questions so you can gain insight into the development that your baby is undergoing and the many changes your partner is experiencing inside her body during this stage of the pregnancy. Such milestones are significant, and it is vital that you both share them with one another. Hearing your unborn baby's first heartbeat will change your life. You will begin to see life differently and even have this unconditional love for your unborn child that is beyond anyone you have ever loved in your life (Rodgers, 2020).

Week eleven - Your partner is most likely frequently urinating, and her hormones are triggering this. She might find it challenging to go straight to bed without finding herself needing to urinate at least twice or three times before going to bed. If she wakes up during the night because she needs to urinate, consider getting nightlights installed in the bathroom and passageway so that your partner does not end up tripping and falling to the ground when she makes her way to the toilet inside the bathroom (Rodgers, 2020).

Week twelve and thirteen - As the first trimester draws to an epic close, some mothers-to-be may not desire to have sex, while others may have a high sex drive. If your partner experiences little to no desire for sex, it would be a great time to think out of the box on ways you can connect with her intimately, such as watching her favorite Netflix series in bed with her favorite snacks. She would even appreciate receiving a bouquet of flowers with a nice message on a card and a surprise spa treatment to get her mind off of things. As for you, if you feel left out, this is normal because pregnancy is heavily felt and experienced by mothers-to-be. But remember, this momentous experience of being pregnant would not have been possible without you - but do not tell your partner this just in case she shouts at you for putting her in this position with aching feet and swollen ankles. If you find her always talking to her sister, mother, or best friend about her pregnancy experience, find a way to get her to confide in you too. Also, do not take it personally that she may be doing this because it may not be intentional. If you do notice this, gently bring it up to her by easing this into a conversation and tell her how this makes you feel when she does it and how much it would mean to you to have her share anything that she wants to talk about concerning the pregnancy (Rodgers, 2020).

Week fourteen - Some expectant fathers who live with their pregnant partner can experience pregnancy symptoms, and this condition is called couvade syndrome or sympathetic pregnancy. Several theories explain this condition, but it has not been identified as a medical condition or a mental health problem (Villines, 2019). Fun fact: Almost fifty percent of all fathers-to-be mimic the pregnancy symptoms of the mother of their unborn child. For example, you might find yourself craving a packet of Lay's Salt and Vinegar flavored potato chips at 2 am or uncontrollably crying while watching a dog food commercial. So, yes, you may be acting more strangely than usual. But it is because you have couvade syndrome and nothing else; if you do not find yourself going through this, it is nothing to worry about (Rodgers, 2020).

Week fifteen - Are you thinking about what names you will give your unborn child? Some helpful tips in deciding what to name your child include things such as going through baby names by each letter of the alphabet and seeing if you find a name that you think would suit your child. Alternatively, you can get creative with it. Perhaps think about merging family names. For example, if your mother's name was Zeta and her maiden name was Richmond, your little one's name could be Zeta Richmond, and their third name will be your family name. If you do not like this combination or any other names you have found, perhaps you can wait until your baby is born to find the name with the right fit (Rodgers, 2020).

Week sixteen - Do you find you have conflicting emotions? One minute you might be feeling over the moon with joy and excitement. And then the next, you might be feeling doubtful about your potential of being a great father to your child. Find someone you can trust to talk to about those anxieties, or better yet, you can share them with your mother-to-be. You might find it beneficial to connect with fellow parents-to-be to form something, like a support group for both yourself and your partner, along your pregnancy journey. Also, you could choose to connect with parents who can guide you and let you know what it truly feels like to be a parent. A great place to start looking for parents to connect with is utilizing social media and even in your neighborhood or the workplace (Rodgers, 2020).

Week seventeen - Your partner may start experiencing a stuffy nose and snoring at night and pressing the snooze button too often during this week and the next couple of weeks. Luckily, this is only temporary. Also, to help mitigate the effects of snoring at night and potentially her snoring waking you up, you can get a humidifier. It will help to unblock her nostrils by clearing out her mucous membranes with excess mucus, which will cause her to sneeze a lot. Alternatively, you can get extra pillows in the bedroom that she can use to elevate her head whenever she wants to sleep (Rodgers, 2020).

Week eighteen - Your partner would greatly appreciate you playing chef in the kitchen since they could be experiencing heartburn at this stage of the pregnancy. It is vital to pay attention to what foods she might be eating that could be causing her to have heartburn, and it is just as crucial to take note of foods that can cause heartburn so that you both do not add them to the menu on the dinner table. For example, very spicy or greasy foods are foods that should be off the menu. She should be eating meals that are digestible yet quick, easy to make, and delicious. At this time, keep dinner very simple as she will be feeling very bogged down and dealing with heartburn, and if you schedule dinner for an earlier time, she would appreciate that (Rodgers, 2020).

Week nineteen - During pregnancy, estrogen and testosterone levels in men are lower than usual. And if you find yourself almost wanting to shed a tear at the sight of baby shoes or outfits, know it is nature's way of preparing you to be nurturing and caring towards your baby. Typically, your hormone levels will return to their normal levels about six months when the baby has arrived and has settled into their new life and home (Rodgers, 2020). For now, enjoy the ride!

Week twenty - The ultrasound this week, known as the 20-week anatomy scan, will be more detailed, and the doctor will be able to tell you how your baby is growing. It is possible to get a sonogram that you can show your family and friends. This picture will document a monumental milestone of the pregnancy and something you can always look back on and remember the pregnancy journey to this point (Rodgers, 2020).

Week twenty-one - Mothers-to-be often start feeling their baby become active. It is that time when the baby starts kicking or moving a lot, which lets the mother-to-be know there is a tiny human being growing and developing a personality of their own inside her. Seeing that little hand or foot kick your partner's belly is an exciting pregnancy milestone. If you want to have your baby show more movement, you can get the mother-to-be to snack on healthy foods, high in carbohydrates and protein, or lie down on the sofa. The blood sugar from the food and the relaxation from lying down will get the baby to be active (Rodgers, 2020).

Week twenty-two - Some pregnant women often prefer to abstain from sex during pregnancy because they feel less attractive and uncomfortable having sex with the baby inside of them. And then some fathers-to-be are afraid of harming their unborn child during sex. As long as the doctor of the mother-to-be medically gives her permission to proceed with engaging in sexual activity, you can go ahead and have fun with it. Your baby is safe in the womb and will not be able to see or feel anything going on between you and their mother-to-be. Also, you will not be able to reach them in the womb. It would be worthwhile to find positions that work for her and the belly. Alternately, you could explore new ways to show your love for her (Rodgers, 2020).

Week twenty-three - If you start noticing that the mother of your child is having trouble falling asleep, express your empathy. You can get her a full-body pillow to help her fall asleep more easily and comfortably. Alternatively, you could engage her in intimate pillow talk that leads to lovemaking - well, even better, you both would have hit the jackpot! Hopefully, it will help her fall asleep (Rodgers, 2020).

Week twenty-four - Your baby would be the equivalent size of an orange now. Those little ears will be able to pick up the effects of sounds from the outside world. A great tool to bond with your baby would be to play your favorite songs for them regularly. You have probably seen some parents-to-be placing headphones on the belly of the mother-to-be and playing music. When the baby arrives, you can use those songs to soothe them when they start uncontrollably crying, and perhaps you do not know what you can do to calm them down (Rodgers, 2020).

Week twenty-five - The mother-to-be, at this point, would have been able to feel her baby move inside of her, but now she will be able to see their movements outside her belly, too. By week twenty-five or twenty-six, you can ask if you can place your hand on her pregnant belly to try to feel and see the energetic moves of your baby-to-be (Rodgers, 2020). Now from experiencing this, do you believe in miracles?

Week twenty-six - By this week and the following, the second trimester will be drawing to a close soon. So, you may find yourself thinking about the delivery. Labor may be a scary thought for you. But if you know what to expect, you will not feel as scared anymore. It is advisable to read about childbirth and go to your nearest hospital to get a sense of where to go when your partner goes into labor. You can choose to do the tour of the hospital either online or physically. Also, you should have a trial run of driving to the hospital and check for the fastest route to get there. You can even enroll in child birthing classes to learn about everything that happens during labor and get more vital information about parenting in those first couple of months when the baby is born and more helpful information. You could also chat to new parents who would have great information too (Rodgers, 2020).

Week twenty-seven - The mother-to-be will be getting stretch marks that will become drier and more difficult to resist the urge to scratch. Unfortunately, scratching will make the stretch marks worse and will not provide her with the relief she desires from the itchiness caused by the dryness. So, how about you get her some shea butter or coconut cream to smear on her belly? That will help moisturize the skin and reduce the appearance of stretch marks. She would appreciate getting pampered with a massage all over her pregnant belly and caressing her other body parts that might be swollen or aching (Rodgers, 2020).

Week twenty-eight - As the third trimester begins, the mother-to-be would have probably given some thought to whether to feed the baby formula or breastmilk. Set the time to talk about it with her and conduct research on the benefits of breastfeeding if you do not know them already. For example, receiving breast milk will help the baby have a lower risk of feeling sick, and the mother will lower her chances of getting breast cancer later on in her life. Some mothers cannot breastfeed for medical reasons or prefer not to breastfeed their baby. Instead, they want to use formula. Whether you choose to use breastfeeding or formula, skin and eye contact is beneficial to optimal brain development and will help the mother bond with her baby (Rodgers, 2020).

Week twenty-nine - With eleven weeks left, you might be having difficulty falling asleep just like your partner. The reason might have something to do with thinking about the things you will no longer be able to do once your baby comes home with you from the hospital. Maybe you enjoy going hiking whenever you like, checking out new restaurants in town, and painting the city red when you go out clubbing with your friends. Transmute these thoughts and start thinking about what you will have once the baby arrives - you will have this cute, tiny, beautiful human being you can share your life with your partner. Yes, life will be very different from what you are used to as there will be many changes and sacrifices that you both will have to make for this new bundle of joy, but it will all be worth it, and life will be sweeter than pie (Rodgers, 2020).

Week thirty - Counting down, ten weeks left now. The birthing process might be troubling you at this time. If so, find a childbirth class that you could still enroll in. The nearest hospital your partner will most likely deliver your baby at should have a childbirth class that you can enroll yourself in at this time. Also, this would be a great time to discuss a birthing plan with the mother of your unborn child. That will consist of whether she would want to receive an epidural during giving birth, whom she wants to be in the delivery room as she is in labor, and make decisions about who will cut the umbilical cord. You will need to chip in as much as you can to get your voice heard as the father-to-be but do it diplomatically even though she will have the majority of the say since she is the one who will be in labor and needs to give birth to your baby. After the both of you come up with a birthing plan, have several copies available. You will need to take a few copies to the hospital to give her doctor to put them into her medical records (Rodgers, 2020).

Week thirty-one - Your baby has grown immensely from being the size of an orange a couple of weeks ago to now a coconut. Even though this growth is beautiful and miraculous, the pregnancy will be taking its toll on your partner's body. She will have to make accommodations such as shifting her posture, and the brain fog of being pregnant is making her clumsy and making it difficult for her to focus on day-to-day activities and tasks. It is a great time to tape down carpets or rugs that you have in your home and install handles next to the shower to ensure that she does not end up tripping and falling accidentally because of being a klutz as a result of the brain fog from the pregnancy (Rodgers, 2020).

Week thirty-two - Schedule an appointment with your doctor to ensure your immunizations are up to date. When the baby arrives, you must protect them from illnesses such as flu and pertussis (i.e., commonly known as whooping cough, which is a very contagious respiratory infection tract), which can cause serious health complications for newborn babies. Also, many newborn babies catch whooping cough from their immediate family members. Although you may have gotten the Tdap immunization you got while a child, you will need to get a booster shot before your child arrives. Also, consider getting the flu vaccine because your baby will thank you when they are healthy and thriving (Rodgers, 2020). While you are thinking about this, schedule your visit to the doctor as soon as possible - do not wait!

Week thirty-three - As you are scheduling your own doctor's appointment, it is advisable that you think about actively seeking a doctor for your baby too. You can look into asking your new network of soon-to-be parents or experienced parents from your neighborhood or on social media which pediatricians they would recommend you to use for your child. Alternatively, you could conduct a Google search to find pediatricians close to you and have read their reviews. Also, you could ask your partner's doctor for some recommendations - they might even have some good ones. When you find a couple of pediatricians that you like, look into whether they accept your medical insurance and then devise a list of questions to ask them. These questions could be about their childrearing philosophy and whether they allow people to call them after work hours (Rodgers, 2020).

Week thirty-four - Spend some time together packing an overnight bag to prepare when you need it in a couple of weeks when you go to the hospital. It will help you ensure that you have everything she will need in that bag. If you choose to gather stuff at the last minute, there will be essential items you and she will forget amidst the panic and excitement when she starts getting contractions and it is time to get her to the hospital. Consider talking about the personal items your partner needs to be in the overnight bag, and once this process is complete, check that everything is in the bag that must be there. You might also want to prepare for the possibility of staying at the hospital for over 24 hours. So, pack some clean clothes that you can wear the following day and do not forget to take some toiletries with you - you will need them, especially when you have to be at the hospital overnight. Also, some other essential items include snacks, phone chargers, and tablets to keep you entertained by watching movies in case your partner is in labor for many hours (Rodgers, 2020). The distraction will serve you both well.

Week thirty-five - You must have seen those births that generally happen at the side of the road in the backseat, which the traffic cop attends to around midnight or the early morning that appear on movies and in the news. You might even be thinking that it could be you and your partner, especially if she goes into labor late at night. To prepare for this small probability if it were to happen, it would be wise to ensure you have gas in the car, the quickest routes to the hospital on your phone, and keep a blanket, towels, and bottled water in the trunk of the car - just in case. You could consider doing a practice run of using the quickest routes to the hospital that you have on your phone again to get a sense of the traffic flow and assess whether there is any construction going on along the routes (Rodgers, 2020).

Week thirty-six - Now, your baby could arrive at any moment in these next four weeks. If your baby were to arrive during this week of the pregnancy cycle, the doctors would consider them premature. If you have not already thought about letting your employer know that you are soon going to be expecting a baby, then this would be a great time to do so. You should let your employer know this and ask whether they can let you work close to home, especially if you travel a long distance from home to work and vice versa. If your employer does not allow you to work remotely or close to home, ask them for leniency regarding running out of the office without notice when you get the phone call that your partner has gone into labor. Hopefully, your employer will be compassionate and understanding of the unpredictability of your partner going into labor at any time and anywhere in these next four weeks. You could think about putting in the extra time now since you will soon need to take time off when the baby arrives (Rodgers, 2020).

Week thirty-seven - You might be experiencing some pre-delivery nervousness at this time that could be causing you to clean out closets that are more than full to their capacity. Also, you could be organizing cabinets that you know you need to throw away things that you do not need anymore. The pantry and basement are other places that might be attracting your attention to clear stuff you do not have any use for anymore and want to clean. Your nesting instincts are starting to develop, and this is nature's way to prepare you and ensure you will have a clean and comfortable environment when the baby arrives soon. Do not be shocked by the transformation; just let yourself clean and organize the cabinets as much as you want, even if it is in the odd hours of the morning. Just watch out that your soon-to-be mother of your child is not overdoing it with her compulsive nesting instincts because she will get fatigued very quickly at this stage of her pregnancy (Rodgers, 2020).

Week thirty-eight - Your unborn child is the same size as a watermelon at this point, and even her growing belly resembles it. Love-making may be on both of your minds. However, perhaps the thought of the possibility of inducing labor may be preventing you both from engaging in the act of love. But if her doctor has not cautioned you against engaging in love-making, then it should not be a problem, and enjoy yourselves. Actually, with the doctor's okay, you can have sex until the end of the trimester (Rodgers, 2020).

Week thirty-nine - You have less than a week left until your baby arrives! As the due date nears and she could go into labor at any time now, take some time to enjoy the last couple of moments being a family of only two people by doing things that you have not done in a while as a couple. Because sooner than you can say "Hi baby," you will have a family of three or more if you are expecting twins or triplets or even quadruplets. If you have been working on the nursery, you could do that together. But get your partner to do some stress-free things, such as picking out colors, patterns, furniture, and decorations for the nursery - no heavy lifting. Also, you could have a lunch date on the beach or book her into a hotel for the weekend and pamper her with room service and spa treatments in her hotel room. Or, you could take her to the park for a stroll before the sunset. Or, you could do all of these leisure activities or think of something else that would be a fun and relaxing date (Rodgers, 2020).

Week forty - Is your baby not here yet? No worries, about thirty percent of pregnant women come to the end of their third trimester without giving birth. They tend to go over their due date for a couple of days and even weeks, and your partner could fall under this category of expectant mothers. If this does happen, you need to remain calm and relaxed so that she is too. Some best advice would be to call or text your family and closest friends who would be wondering or awaiting the news of the baby's arrival. Let them know you will call them when the baby has arrived, and you would appreciate them giving you space at this time. In the meanwhile, install the baby seat in the car, ensure the nursery is ready for the baby, fold the baby's clothes and tidy up the toys you have probably bought for the baby to play with in the playpen. You could also freeze up a couple of easy-to-make dishes that you can heat quickly once the baby comes home with you from the hospital. When they get here, you will not want to stand at the stove and cook for forty-five minutes to an hour because you will be tired and need your rest (Rodgers, 2020).

Week forty-one - A study conducted by Brown and Davies (2014) on one hundred and seventeen dad's experiences of being supportive of breastfeeding over the past two years have become fathers to newborn babies. In the study, they voluntarily agreed to fill out an open-ended questionnaire. The open-ended questionnaire asked questions that aimed to get an in-depth understanding of their postnatal experiences of being supportive of breastfeeding, the education and support they obtained, and any ideas they had to improve breastfeeding education and promotion for fathers in the future. The study revealed that many fathers were supportive of their partner's decision to breastfeed their babies but felt helpless at practically supporting their partner in the breastfeeding process (Brown & Davies, 2014). You know what? If you happen to get frustrated with the postnatal breastfeeding support that you cannot provide because you feel like it is limited or even inconsequential, just know that your encouragement of your partner's breastfeeding is significant because ninety-six percent of mothers report being willing to start breastfeeding and even continuing with it. So, take up the role of being your partner's breastfeeding cheerleader with pride, and when the baby has arrived, ask the nurse to give you advice and tips on breastfeeding. When you return home from the hospital and begin to settle into your new life, and your partner begins to breastfeed your baby, ensure there are always snacks and water close to her because breastfeeding can take its toll on the female body (Rodgers, 2020). Occasionally, when she is done feeding the baby, try taking the child and helping them burp while your partner eats or takes a nap. It is one practical idea that you could use to support your partner.

Week forty-two - You could have worrying thoughts at the back of your mind or have mind chatter, such as "My baby is well past their due date and may have some birth defects." Due dates are only a guide for the doctors to know when you could expect the baby's arrival, which can always be roughly off by a couple of days or weeks. Rest assured that your baby is doing well and your partner's doctor is keeping tabs to ensure everything is fine with the baby and the mother-to-be. During this time, you could see if you have items that might be short and need stocking in the fridge and the pantry. Then, while you are at it, you can buy essential items the nursery needs that you might not have been able to get, such as a cradle, a baby monitor, a rocking chair, and a diaper changing dresser. When you have finished all of this, relax and await your baby's arrival, which should not be too far in the future now (Rodgers, 2020).

As a new parent, you will want to listen to every possible source of information from anywhere and everywhere when faced with a problem. Basil, a new father, shared that his baby boy struggled to latch and feed properly, and he mentioned he soon went into problem-solving mode. But he noticed that he and his wife were listening to too many people and just needed to let nature take its course. After a few months or so, his boy could feed properly. So, the lesson in Basil's story is to listen to your intuition or nesting instincts as a parent because it is always right. And sometimes, some problems only require nature to do its thing and have faith in that (Family Action, 2020).

Chapter 2:

Building a Healthy Relationship With the Mother of Your Unborn Child

One of the hardest things about parenting is that you just never know what the outcome will be. It's a total leap of faith. — Catherine Newman

Becoming parents to a child is a challenging job. Both parents must have a healthy parenting relationship that will work for them and find ways to improve their parenting relationship with time. One of the ways to do this is through identifying the positive and celebrating the things that are going superbly well in the parenting relationship and continuously making room for improvement. And refrain from dwelling on the negative too much. Such negativity, for example, faulting the mother for what she is not doing for the child, being hard on yourself for mistakes you have made, and even feeling guilty for focusing on your career instead of being there more for your child. If you are a dutiful father and your child knows and feels your love for them, pat yourself on the back because you are doing a great job thus far (Wolf, 2020).

So, to continue being the great father to your newborn baby, there are tools you will need to nurture a healthy parenting relationship. These include but are not limited to conflict resolution and going to therapy to work on yourself. Conflict resolution is a great strategy to help build a healthy, long-lasting parenting relationship with your partner. Going to therapy can help resolve all negative emotions and experiences you may be holding onto from the past that you need to release to become the best version of yourself. As you read through these different factors for building a healthy parenting relationship, you might want to think about what you can take away from these and use in your parenting relationship (Wolf, 2020).

Establish healthy boundaries - It is respectful to know and abide by the limits that both of you set and to recognize what lines both of you need to honor to have a healthy and productive parenting relationship. It will help to establish balance in your child's life by having parents who know how to communicate effectively and come together when their child needs them while respecting each other's boundaries and loving one another. It will set a good precedent for your child to see you both supportive of each other's role in their life and learning to put your differences aside and prioritize your child's care and wellbeing (Wolf, 2020).

Set up a timetable collaboratively to take care of your child's needs - With busy schedules and taking care of your own needs as parents, it is best to set up a timetable that both of you agree to uphold. It will help usher you into your new life as you begin to prioritize the needs of your child but also assist you to learn not to compromise too much on your schedule, especially if you happen to pick up this habit. Also, it will make the adjustment process to becoming a first-time dad a little bit easier. If you are struggling to deal with the different things that may be going on in your life when the baby has arrived, seek mental health support or confide in a trusted friend. Also, it is always best to transition into your new life with a newborn already having had these conversations about how your life will be like with your partner because your life as it used to be will never be the same again when you have them in your life. Hence, communication, trust, and commitment are the foundation for a healthy parenting relationship whether the parents are dating, married, or exes. It is vital to maintain effective communication, rely on one another with confidence, and do what you say you will do and when you can do it with devotion to your child. Also, you should know that setting up routines does not make it a constant. Things can always change because life is not static, and life's circumstances can bring changes to predetermined ways of living and plans. But it is still good parenting practice to have one to ensure as parents you are on the same page most of the time and make accommodations for one another if one of you has too much they are dealing with in their lives (Wolf, 2020).

Willingness to exercise flexibility when needed - Even though having a schedule is great for both of you, it is always crucial to be accommodating and compassionate towards one another and the things you have going on in your life. There might come a time when you will need your partner to be understanding and step up when too much is going on in your life. You are individuals, despite being parents together, and might not be able to commit to the things you usually do. For example, it may be your turn to take your child to their soccer games on Saturdays or attend their dance recitals on Friday evenings. Please remember this golden principle: Do to others what you would like them to do to you. Demonstrate the courtesy you would like to be in your parenting relationship to effectively manifest an accommodative parenting relationship, whether you are single or married. Focusing on the aspects of their behavior that displeases you will create a hostile, negative relationship and ultimately get you nowhere. Unfortunately, you will be stuck with a disrespectful, self-centered, and, at worst, they could become a controlling partner you will have to interact with for the rest of your life (Wolf, 2020).

John Cecil is a single parent from the United Kingdom who has 50/50 shared custody of his child with his ex. In his blog article titled "My success in co-parenting," he discusses his journey of working on himself to be a better father and co-parent. The amount of work he put into building a healthy co-parenting relationship with his ex is inspirational. Some of the strategies he used to ensure co-parenting works with his ex-partner was using a Google calendar to schedule everything. He makes it a point to prioritize spending time with his daughter, knowing what he needs to do, and always being present for his daughter's milestones. He also mentioned that he appreciates the time his child spends with her mother because it gives him time to socialize, and being away from her, even if it is a short while, makes his heart grow fonder for her even more. Being accommodating has been one of the foundational principles for John's successful co-parenting story as he says, "We have our set dates and it works for us. We make it a point though, that if one of us wants her on a date that is not ours, for whatever reason, we try to accommodate. Holidays are tough sometimes, but we work through it. If one of us [is] sick or needs to be out of town, we step up for each other. If I need to take off work early to pick up my daughter from school, I try to make it work. If there is a party that the both of them have been invited to, I allow it. When my family has a Saturday dinner, not on my weekend, I ask for that time." Having an agreement as parents that you will always do what is best for your child and enrich their childhood experiences with joyous memories, putting your pride aside, and showing goodwill to your partner, is a recipe for great parenting (Cecil, 2019).

Deferring caregiving responsibilities to your partner before anyone else - You may have family members who may want to involve themselves in the way you parent your child and in the ins and outs of your parenting relationship with your partner. That can negatively impact your ability to cultivate a collaborative, healthy parenting relationship with the mother of your child. When that happens, it can be annoying and frustrating. You may even find yourself deferring caregiving responsibilities to them before your partner, which can cause problems with the mother of your child. Woolfall et al. (2015) conducted a study on how parents and health care workers experienced clinical care research without deferred consent for emergency treatments involving children with life-threatening illnesses in twelve children's hospitals in the United Kingdom. The results revealed that some of the two hundred and seventy-five parents were shocked to find out that their child either had or could have potentially enrolled into a CATheter infection in Children (CATCH) trial without their consent. Even some health care workers were apprehensive about enrolling these children in this trial without parental consent. The study concluded that deferred consent in pediatric emergency settings is a practice that can be supported, but discussions with parents about it must be appropriately conducted and communicated within the due course (Woolfall et al., 2015). This study relates to how parents should have the courtesy to ask each other whether the other can take care of the child. If they need to be somewhere urgently or they may have double booked themselves, instead of perhaps calling a babysitter to look after their child at home, first check-in with your partner (Wolf, 2020).

Agreeability: Learning to compromise - Reaching common ground can be difficult when you see things differently based on culture, religion, ethnicity, class, and gender. Decisions that you both make about your child will require lots of compromising and being open to seeing things from the point of view of the other parent. It is always great to remind yourselves that you must put the child's best interests first, no matter what.

Work on agreeing on the most crucial aspects of your child's upbringing, such as their education, religious beliefs, healthy eating habits, discipline, socially acceptable behavior, personal hygiene, manners, mental health care, and building their self-esteem and confidence. Devising a parenting plan might be helpful to do whether you do it before childbirth or when the baby has arrived (Wolf, 2020).

Being a first-time dad, you must know that you play a vital role in your child's life, and the mother of your baby is just as important in your child's life, and they are blessed to have both of you willing to raise them and give them the love they deserve. Do not take each other for granted, and work hard to build and maintain a healthy parenting relationship with the mother of your child. When your child is older, they will love you for it when they reflect on the good times they experienced during their childhood years. And remember how you modeled a healthy relationship with their mother despite all the challenges and disagreements you had in your relationship over the years (Wolf, 2020).

Chapter 3:

Connecting With Your

Unborn Child

Children will not remember you for the material things you gave them but for the feeling that you cherished them. –Richard L. Evans

It is wise to bond with your unborn baby to get better acquainted. A study conducted by Alio et al. (2013) defines the 'ideal' involved father during pregnancy as a male counterpart who is holistically present, easy to contact, and makes themselves available to tend to anything related to the needs of the mother-to-be and their baby. Also, they are compassionate, interested in learning about the stages of pregnancy, and feel a sense of pride in providing emotional, physical, and financial support to the mother of their unborn child (Alio et al., 2013). There are many creative, fun ideas, as mentioned below, you could use to be perceived as this 'ideal' involved father, and bonding with your baby-to-be while they are still developing in your partner's pregnant belly is one of the ways.

Sonogram Art - At the first prenatal doctor visit you attended, the doctor gave you a sonogram, a picture which was the first glimpse of your baby - do you happen to remember what you did with it? Do you remember where you put it? If you still have this picture, you could turn it into a work of art. If you are interested in doing this: Firstly, you will need to convert the picture into digital form if you have a physical or hard copy of it. You can also check your emails; perhaps the doctor sent this sonogram to your inbox? When you have a digital copy of your sonogram, get creative with it. You can add filters, beautiful quotes about fatherhood, and even include some emojis to showcase your sense of humor and give it some personality. You can think about documenting your memories of the pregnancy journey through scrapbooking. So, when your baby is old enough, you can show them how it felt like when you saw them for the first time on a sonogram, and you can consider capturing the most significant memories you have with them too in your scrapbook. If you are a sentimental person, you could buy a locket and add this creative image of the sonogram on both halves and gift it to your partner - perhaps at the end of the third trimester. It will be something special to do to commemorate this beautiful journey (Gordon, 2013).

Picture the world of adventure you will have with your baby - Typically, mothers-to-be picture their baby as a baby rather than imagining the adventures they will have with them, which dads-to-be generally do. So, what is the first adventure you would like to do with your baby? If you enjoy hiking, you could buy the smallest size of hiking boots and think about when you would be able to go with them to your favorite hiking spot. Remember to take pictures and videos as your child may not remember you took them on their first hike when they were a baby. But how reminiscent do you think it would be in five years to look back on these memories, which you would have documented on a video camera, and tell them a story about this adventure? That would be cool, right? It is beautiful to dream of the activities you would like to do with them as they grow up. Alternatively, you can purchase or create little souvenirs that are related to those activities that can serve the role of cementing your bond with your child. Since they will be new to this crazy place we call the world, they would relish going on adventures with their old man, and when your child turns eighteen years old, hopefully, they will want to paint the city red with their best friend of all time. Their connection to you as their father is something no money could ever buy, and it will be one of the things they will cherish the most in their lives - having an involved, caring, and loving father (Gordon, 2013).

Reading books to the baby bump - Read, read, read to your partner's belly! I am sure you have some books from your childhood or even your adulthood that you would not mind your child knowing about since you love those books. If you do not have any books you want to share with your baby, ask your partner if she has suggestions of books you could read to her belly. It may feel strange to read to your baby-to-be in your partner's belly. But by the third trimester, they would already have developed ears and be able to hear sounds, actually from week sixteen onwards, and you can get an early start with influencing their choices of literature. Moreover, you can read the New York Times bestselling children's books to get them ahead with the good stuff. And who knows, they could be the next

Julia Quinn or Williams Shakespeare who will have a deep love for writing and English literature. Reading will be something they will grow up to love to do because you read to them while they were in their mother's womb. Also, think about making a collection of your favorite children's books as you come to find them and choose to read them to your baby. Reading to your baby is a wonderfully practical way to get involved in the pregnancy. Hopefully, when your child is old enough to choose their books, they might gravitate towards the books you used to read when they were in their mother's womb - that would be such a full-circle moment when that happens (Gordon, 2013).

Singing to the baby bump - This might be presumptuous, but I am guessing you are a music lover, right? You can gather some of your family members together and have a fun night singing karaoke to your baby in your partner's belly. Your baby will be able to hear the musical sounds and the beautiful singing voices. Remember from two or three weeks into the second trimester as the sounds will be able to move past the amniotic fluid. Surprisingly, as you and your partner spend time singing to your baby while they are in your partner's belly, they will be able to recognize their parents' voices and some of the songs you used to play for them, which can serve to calm them down when they are crying and need something soothing to relax them. A family that harmonizes together will stay together through the highs and lows (Gordon, 2013).

Becoming a father for the first time will transform you. You may want to provide your child with the things you lacked when growing up. Those things might have been security, having play dates with friends at their homes, having your parents read to you every night before bed, a house with a big yard to play with your toys and friends, or even being there in ways that your father was not for you when you were growing up. When you come to experience fatherhood, especially for the first time, you will have parenting instincts that will make you want to go beyond only being a provider and protector, which is all good. But you may notice yourself becoming more tender-hearted and emotional just like this father of two; Glenn Egamino says, "I'm surprised by how much fatherhood has changed me - I've grown to be much more patient and just enjoy the little things in life. I've also become much more sensitive, and have a softer heart. Being greeted at the door by your kids after a long day of work is one of the best feelings. Fatherhood has shown me a love that I never knew existed" (Toub, 2021).

Chapter 4:

Birthing Plans

It's the most profound gift and the most daunting challenge. —
Matt Bomer

There are many expectations you might have from delivery. A birth plan can help you, the healthcare professional, and the mom-to-be know what to consider, include and expect in the delivery room. In modern times, birth plans are becoming more and more popular. Millennial parents-to-be are using their power more than ever when it comes to having their voices heard in what they expect in the delivery room with their doctor and medical staff of the hospital. You can work on making a well-thought-out birth plan from scratch. Or, you can get an online version of it by searching for birth plan templates. Thinking everything through concerning the childbirth will give you and your partner a sense of reassurance, control, and stability on the day of delivery. Constructing birth plans with your healthcare professional will allow you to advocate for your care pertaining to issues that you may not be given much say in, for example, augmentation of labor or pain management options during birth. If you choose to go the route of using online birthing plan templates, there are some details you will find in this chapter that may not be included in those online templates, which will prove to be helpful, and you would want to discuss with your partner (Coleman, 2020).

If you were to meet with an obstetrician, they would tell you there are many ways your baby can be born into this world. It is best to empower yourself and work together to determine the perfect childbirth instead of leaving it to your healthcare professional in the hospital or the midwife. A birth plan helps you and your partner determine where you want the birth to take place, how you want it to feel, whom you want to be there, and even how you want the atmosphere to be (Coleman, 2020).

A general birth plan checklist will consist of the following questions:

Whom do you want in the delivery room?

Do you want a doula to be present in the room?

Do you have a birthing position or style that you prefer, for example, a water or home birth?

How will you manage pain during childbirth?

Will you have your doctor monitor your baby and partner's fetal heart rate during labor?

What kind of atmosphere do you want in your room regarding music, lighting, and decorations?

Will you have on special clothing?

Are you willing to have the doctor perform an episiotomy to allow the baby to come through the vagina easier?

Would you want to delay cutting the umbilical cord?

Do you wish the father to be the third hand that "catches" your baby with the doctor?

Whom do you want to cut the umbilical cord?

How will you document the birthing process?

Do you wish to immediately breastfeed and have skin to skin contact after childbirth?

Do you expect the hospital, the birthing center, or the midwife to take care of your partner directly after birth?

Are there any special requests you might have for your baby's care?

Do you want to have the placenta?

If a cesarean must be performed by the doctor and the hospital's medical staff, do you have any particular requests?

A birth plan is a document between one and two pages and at most three pages that foregrounds what the parents-to-be ideally want the birthing process to be like for them. Birth plans, as you would have noticed from the checklist above, cover a slew of options, and these range from the loved ones you want to be in the room with you and the person you want to have the honors at cutting the umbilical cord. Also, the mood and the vibe of the room (relating to having music, some fairy lights, and essential oils, for example) and whether you want to have your baby immediately breastfeed and have skin to skin contact for bonding to take place quickly. Also, as a first-time dad, discussing your involvement in the birthing process is crucial for you to feel helpful in that moment (Coleman, 2020).

Some tips for creating a birth plan with your partner are:

Offer your partner the opportunity to share their wishes regarding each option you will be discussing. As her birth partner, only show your emotional and physical support instead of being demanding or too opinionated.

Make your intentions known about how involved you wish to be in childbirth. You only have one birth to be present for each of your children, and each one is special. Since this will be your first birth, confidently share how much you want to have an active role in the childbirth of your first child.

Construct your birth plan together and once it is complete, make an appointment with your doctor to discuss it with them to ensure it is practical and safe.

Before the birth, make sure to print several copies of the birth plan. The doctor, your partner, the delivery room nurse, the birthing center, or the midwife should at least have their copy, and have an extra one in your pocket just in case someone loses theirs. The birth plan will act as a guide as the birthing process takes place (Coleman, 2020).

Ideally, aim to have a joint discussion with your partner about the birthing plan at the beginning of the third trimester and once it is complete, discuss it with the doctor by week thirty-four when your partner goes for her prenatal checkups. It would be unfortunate to have this master birth plan not executed because it could not be discussed with your doctor in time. Usually, some doctors allow expectant mothers to give birth around the thirty-fourth week. Doctors will never put a stop to childbirth because no birth plan was discussed before the birth took place. Luckily, that leaves you ample time to think and discuss what you want your birth plan to be like with your partner's doctor. If you enroll in a childbirth class, you will have the benefit of receiving access to a birthing template that will be according to the birthing method you and your partner would like to have for your childbirth (Coleman, 2020). For instance, a home birth, vaginal delivery, water birth, hospital delivery, Lamaze or Bradley method, or assisted births such as a C-section, vacuum extraction, or forceps delivery (Oberg, 2022). There are good birthing plan templates you can find on the internet, which can guide you and your partner towards having the childbirth of your dreams if nature allows it. Soon you will hear a story from a second-time father below that will let you know that childbirth can be rather unpredictable and prepare for anything to happen (Coleman, 2020).

A study conducted by Ledenfors and Berterö (2016) aimed to recognize and describe manifest meanings of first-time fathers' experiences of normal childbirth. The primary investigators used qualitative interviews to collect their data. The study utilized eight first-time dads and interviewed them about two to six after the birthing process. The study was set in Sweden, and the interviews took place in both urban and rural areas. The study revealed that the birthing process was a transformative experience for the first-time dads as they felt wide-ranging emotions during the birth, which they had never felt before. They felt helpless during childbirth because they could not provide their partner with the support they needed, and seeing their partner in pain made them feel vulnerable at that moment.

Also, the role of fathers during childbirth should be seen as a unit with their partner because the father-to-be can provide reassurance, security, strength, and care to the mother-to-be, and that should be recognized before and during the childbirth. Seeing their child for the first time was expressed as a significant encounter. These first-time dads felt a sense of relief that the pain their partner was experiencing was over, and typically they considered whether their child was healthy. The most beautiful feeling was when they witnessed their baby put on the mother's breast for feeding, and this feeling was similar to falling in love. They feel this beautiful sense of nervousness and a strong parenting instinct to nurture their baby and pure happiness (Ledenfors & Berterö, 2016).

You will find that your partner will be mostly focused on the birth process more than anything else. In your birth plan, you can include specific birthing positions that you wish to use, whether you want a doula to be present or the doctor should not perform an episiotomy and have a particular pain relief method. The doctor will go accordingly with this birth plan when the birth takes place. Even though you may not be the one who is giving birth to your child as the father, however, there are several ways to be actively involved in childbirth, such as "catching" your baby with the doctor and cutting the umbilical cord. Also, you can help the clinical staff with weighing and measuring them and giving your baby their first bath after 6 hours if possible (Coleman, 2020).

No one can confidently predict that everything will go as planned. Hence, it is vital to be flexible as the staff involved with ensuring this birth is a success will try by all means to follow the birth plan to meet your expectations and desires. But anything can change at any moment during the birth, and you will need to prepare yourself mentally for such a thing and talk about any changes which occur to the original birth plan with your doctor if time allows (Coleman, 2020).

Mo Mulla tells his story of delivering his baby at home for the first time. Oh my goodness - it was an unplanned home birth that went perfectly well! It marked a significant duty as a father that he could have never imagined. Most fathers-to-be never think about the possibility of delivering their own child and how they would handle such a situation. Amid learning about pregnancy development which you are doing as you read about it in the first chapter by picking up this handbook, it is important to consider learning all that you can about delivering a baby. Doing so will give you a strong sense of security, as you will know how to manage the situation and help your partner give birth as comfortably as possible (Mulla, 2022).

Mo Mulla mentions in retelling his story that they did not prepare for a home birth, they planned to have a hospital delivery. His wife had contractions very close to each other and could not get to the hospital because their baby was crowning while they were in the living room of their house, and the paramedics could not reach them fast enough. So, he decided to make the living room as comfortable as he possibly could by placing a couple of cushions and covers on the floor and instructed Google Home to "Play rain sounds." His wife went into active labor quicker than he could say, "I can see the baby's head!" Luckily, before he went to the living room, he noticed his wife was not in bed sleeping next to him, but he found her kneeling halfway to the ground in pain. So, he contacted the paramedics on the phone to ask for an ambulance to come when his wife started experiencing contractions. It was shocking to realize that he was going to have to deliver his baby by himself since the paramedics were taking a long time to get to their home, but he was a champ as he assisted his wife in giving birth to their daughter. So, as his wife was pushing the head first, followed by the tiny shoulders, he supported the baby's head with his hands. As his wife continued to push out the rest of their baby's body, he started to pull the baby's body gently as she was coming out and wrapped her in a fresh towel. His wife delivered their daughter with no pain medication, which deserves praise. They had no direct assistance from paramedics as they arrived late or after the birth. When the paramedics made it to their house, they checked that everything was fine with the baby and the mother, and indeed they were both perfectly healthy. The moral of the story is that childbirth is unpredictable, and you must prepare yourself for any actuality - including assisting with delivering your beautiful baby! (Mulla, 2022).

Chapter 5:

The Arrival of the Baby

I think [fatherhood] changes your relationship with time. I just don't have time to waste. You gotta be really deliberate with how you choose to spend your day, because those are the moments you're away from your child. –Mahershala Ali

Preparing for the arrival of a newborn baby for the first time has numerous factors that one must consider and seek guidance. In this chapter, some tips will be shared about ways you can prepare as a first-time dad and essential items you will need to have to help you transition better into fatherhood (KidsInTheHouse2, 2022).

Open yourself up to continuous learning - There is no manual to raising a child or parenthood. But there are many websites and online resources for different parenting issues. These include raising children until they can go to university, disciplining your child, teaching your child how to manage their time effectively, how to build their confidence, the importance of teaching kids their native language, and more. Parenting is a lifelong commitment that requires a willingness to learn and unlearn habits, letting go of limiting beliefs, prejudices and biases, and anything else that you deem toxic that you would not want your child to be learning from you. There are many people you can reach out to for guidance. Those people include your partner's doctor, anyone in your family with children, and you could look into enrolling in parenting classes that are near your home that can help transition you both better into your new roles as parents (KidsInTheHouse2, 2022). All of these resources can prove helpful, but remember to trust your instinct as a parent and when circumstances that are out of your control occur, have faith that your baby will be okay.

Prepare your household and car - Since this is your first time bringing a baby into your house, there are many things you may need to get from shopping stores, such as storage boxes to store their baby-sized clothes, toys, shoes, and essential items for feeding and diapers. As your baby gets older over the years, you can keep their sporting equipment, photo albums, and old clothes in these storage boxes (KidsInTheHouse2, 2022). You have many essential items you will need to buy, and below is a checklist of those items you will probably need to get in the first three months. That checklist includes essential items for the nursery, day-to-day clothes, feeding, changing diapers, bath time, and equipment to make it easier and safer to travel and walk with them. When you have these items in your arsenal, you will feel ready to start your journey as a parent when you bring your child home from the hospital or when you welcome your baby into the world in your home after a home birth (Pampers, 2021).

The nursery will officially become the most vital room in your entire house once the baby arrives. If you have not bought any essentials for the nursery, you can use this list when shopping for the nursery by yourself or with your partner (Pampers, 2021).

The crib: Buy a crib that will serve multiple purposes to get value for your money because cribs can be expensive. Choose a crib that can convert into a toddler bed, a daybed, and even a full-sized bed. With a crib that can convert into these different types of beds, you can use that same crib for many years, ensure it is safe for the baby to sleep in and a word to the wise make sure to buy a new one (Pampers, 2021).

A crib mattress: Purchase a firm mattress that will fit the crib you have selected for your baby, and it is the best surface for babies to sleep in (Pampers, 2021).

Bedding: Get a waterproof cover and fitted sheets for your crib mattress. Remember to keep your baby's crib free of toys or extra bedding because it will help lessen the probability of your child suffocating by themselves and experiencing sudden infant death syndrome (Pampers, 2021).

Night light: It is pretty handy for feeding and can help you make your way to the nursery in the middle of the night (Pampers, 2021).

Music player: Those songs you used to sing for them while in your partner's pregnant belly, you can play those songs softly to comfort them or soothe them until they fall asleep (Pampers, 2021).

Humidifier: It serves to provide moisture to the air and is helpful for people who live in dry regions with dry air. A humidifier can help make your baby comfortable, especially when they experience coughs or colds (Pampers, 2021).

Rocking chair: Having a rocky chair in the nursery can help with breastfeeding as you can serve as a great spot to do that and even read your baby a bedtime story or sing them a lullaby. The rocking motion is relaxing and can calm your baby if you cuddle them in the chair when they are crying (Pampers, 2021).

Pacifier: Depending on your baby's temperament, you may want to buy a pacifier as one of the ways you can use to soothe them. Be mindful of where you put them because they can get lost or disappear very easily, and quickly. Also, get an age-appropriate pacifier for your baby (Pampers, 2021).

Even though your newborn may be too young to play games right at this moment, here are some toys and gear for playtime that you could buy for your newborn:

Baby swing: A baby swing is another tool you can use to soothe your baby, and the settings control the swaying movement instead of the baby needing to move their legs. Also, baby swings have minimum and maximum weight requirements. Kindly check if you are buying a swing that suits your baby's size. You may find that you can play music from the overhead of the swings (Pampers, 2021).

Baby bouncer: It is similar to a baby swing, but it requires the baby to use their legs to bounce it. While working at home during your paternity leave (if you decide to take it), you can place the baby on the bouncer knowing they are safe and entertained. Also, similar to the swing, it has a limit on its minimum and maximum weight requirements. So, check for your baby's size before you go ahead and purchase one.

Portable play yard or playpen: It is a great baby gear item that can help you do the things you want to do in the house while knowing your baby is safe in an enclosed structure, whether they are snoozing or playing with their toys as you move them from one room to the next with you (Pampers, 2021).

Toys: Toys are great for entertainment and supporting your baby's development as they grow. However, please ensure there are no parts of the toys you buy that have a choking warning. For newborns, toys that rattle are recommended. Also, you might want to buy soft toys that make different sounds to spark their curiosity about the various sounds the toys would be making (Pampers, 2021).

Playmat: Your baby will enjoy a couple of minutes of rolling on the floor with their tummy. You can buy a thick, soft, and comfy playmat for their tummy time and stay close to them when they do this to ensure they do not harm themselves accidentally (Pampers, 2021).

In terms of essential items for feeding, they will help to make the process easier, and they are the following:

Burp cloths: It will be helpful to purchase this item for your partner because it will protect her clothing from your baby spitting up the breastmilk (Pampers, 2021).

Nursing cover: This is another item you can purchase for your partner that will cover her and the baby while feeding them. It usually has a strap that your partner can tie around their neck to secure it (Pampers, 2021).

Bibs: This item will protect your baby's clothing from drool and spilled milk (Pampers, 2021).

Baby bottles: Baby bottles are one of the most important essential items. When buying a bottle for your baby, there are two things you will need to consider: 1) Choose a bottle with a bottle liner that will reduce the likelihood of your newborn swallowing too much air, and plastic baby bottles can provide you with this. 2) Choose a bottle with the nipple shape and size your baby will like (Pampers, 2021).

Breast pump: Your partner may prefer a manual or an electric breast pump model that can express milk from both breasts at the same time, or she may not mind a model that pumps one breast at a time. So, ask your partner what kind of model she would like to have (Pampers, 2021).

Bottle warmer: A bottle warmer is a life-changing essential item because it helps with warming the breast milk or formula evenly and at a safe temperature for your baby is such a time-saver (Pampers, 2021).

Milk storage bags: These are usually single-use products that your partner can pump their breast milk into the bag to store instead of using baby bottles to keep the breast milk (Pampers, 2021).

Bottle brush and sterilizer: A bottle brush will help clean the inside of the baby bottle thoroughly and safely for your baby. A bottle sterilizer will sterilize your baby's bottle and the nipple to keep them hygienic. Alternatively, you could hand wash them thoroughly with a dishwashing detergent, or you can put them in the dishwasher (Pampers, 2021).

Bottle-drying rack: You could consider buying a separate drying rack for your baby's bottles in case you find that you do not have space on your dish-drying stand (Pampers, 2021).

Some parents do not like changing diapers. Unfortunately, it is a parenting duty that you will have to fulfill in the first couple of months of your baby's new life. Here is a list of items that you might want to buy to help with those diaper changes:

Changing table: A changing table can be a time-saver because if it has drawers or shelves, you can keep diapers, wipes, and even some clean clothes in it and organized. Also, some changing tables can have straps that can assist you with safely securing your baby on the changing table. Always keep a hand on your baby even when you have fastened them on the changing table as a precautionary measure to ensure they do not fall unexpectedly (Pampers, 2021).

Changing pad: This is a convenient baby item because it helps keep your baby comfortable and your changing table hygienic as you can use wipes to clean its surface, or if it has a cover, you can remove it and put it in the washing machine (Pampers, 2021).

Diapers: These go without saying that you will need them, and plenty of them. Did you know diapers come in different sizes? Well, they do. As a starting point, you can buy a couple of small packs in various sizes and then when the baby is born, you can purchase the right diaper size (Pampers, 2021).

Diaper rash cream: When to go to your next prenatal check-up or your partner's doctor's appointment, ask them for advice on the best cream or ointment to buy for diaper rash. Also, do not worry that your baby will not get a diaper rash too often, but it is best to have it in your nursery just in case when it does happen (Pampers, 2021).

Wipes: You will need wipes to clean your baby's area covered by a diaper (Pampers, 2021).

Washcloths: You can use a soft washcloth to gently wash your baby at bath time (Pampers, 2021).

Diaper pail: Getting a diaper pail may not be essential, but they help trap odors from dirty diapers. If you want to buy this item, you should buy a diaper pail with a unique liner ring (Pampers, 2021).

Regarding clothes, baby clothes are the cutest and most adorable clothing you will ever see. Try not to stick to only buying small-sized clothes because soon enough you will find they no longer fit them. So, consider bigger-sized clothes too when shopping for their clothes. When you dress your baby, you will need to wear one more layer than you wear yourself, unless you live in an area with warm weather. Generally, you will need a swaddle blanket to swaddle your newborn. Since they will spend most of the time sleeping, sleepwear (i.e., pajamas, sleepers, and sleeping sacks) is an essential clothing item. For general wear around the house or going out and about, you can buy hats to protect them from the sun, undershirts, one-piece outfits in different colors, patterns, and textures, t-shirts, leggings, or comfy pants to look stylish. For cold weather, weather fluctuations, or during the autumn and winter seasons, you can purchase pullover sweaters, cardigans or jackets, lots of socks, a couple of booties, knitted hats or caps, snowsuits, and mittens. You can also consider buying special outfits for the holidays or special occasions (Pampers, 2021).

You may find you will only bathe your baby at least three times a week. Initially, you will need to give your baby sponge baths until their umbilical cord stump falls off their belly button. From there onwards, you will need a baby bathtub for bath time. Ensure you purchase one for your baby's size. To bathe them, you can buy a mild soap and shampoo for baby's sensitive skin and a plastic cup to help pour water on your baby and gently wash off the soap and shampoo with washcloths. You will need soft towels to dry them off when you finish bathing them and a baby moisturizer to moisturize their skin to prevent their skin from getting dry patches (Pampers, 2021).

When you are out and about with your baby, there are a couple of essential items you may want to get to make it easier and safer to travel or walk with them.

Car seat: A car seat is probably one of the first essentials you should get before your due date because you will need to place them in it when you come from the hospital if you are planning to have a hospital delivery. Ensure you get a car seat facing the back and meet the latest safety measures and one that will fit your baby's weight and size for comfortability. Once you have gotten one, please have it adequately installed in your car, and it should be rear-facing (Pampers, 2021).

Stroller: There are many different types of strollers you will find when searching for one, whether online or in-person in-stores. A word of advice? Get a stroller with a rain cover for convenience and ensure it meets the latest safety measures (Pampers, 2021).

Baby carrier: It is an item that is very useful for keeping your newborn close to you as you are moving around. There are various baby carriers that you can get on the market, such as wraps, ring slings, pouches, and front and backpacks. Ensure again that it is safe to use for your baby (Pampers, 2021).

Diaper bag: You will be grateful to have a diaper bag that can fit everything you need to change a diaper when far away from your home. Fortunately, they come in different designs. So, you can go for a trendy diaper bag or just a simple, functional one (Pampers, 2021).

Additionally, you may want to cover the windows of your back seats to protect your baby's skin from harmful UV rays from the sun. Also, if you need to leave your baby at a relative's house, you will need to get a portable crib and ensure it meets the latest safety measures. Getting a portable changing pad will help ensure you have a clean surface to change your baby's diapers, and luckily they can roll up and fit perfectly in many diaper bags. And last but not least, do not forget to get a disposable diaper pail that will help keep your baby's dirty diapers wherever you are (Pampers, 2021).

This chapter has provided a list of many essential items you may want to purchase ahead of your baby's arrival. I do not know how well you are taking care of yourself, especially if you are experiencing similar pregnancy symptoms to your partner and taking care of your partner, doing the laundry and house chores, and cooking healthy meals. Take time out of the day to focus on yourself, whether taking a soothing shower or bath with sea salts and lavender a couple of times a week - do it! You can also get advice from your doctor on foods you can eat to feel revitalized and manage fatigue caused by insomnia or restlessness (KidsInTheHouse2, 2022).

As a first-time dad, do not get too bogged down by the information you read, but prepare yourself for the beautiful journey ahead by taking care of yourself first and your partner. When you are ready and the news has settled that you will become a father, you can start planning specific things. These include attending prenatal checkups with your partner, setting up the nursery, buying essential items for the baby, and babyproofing your home. Preparing for your baby's arrival will take time, and you will need to rely on a great support system and your partner as you both navigate this shared journey of parenthood (KidsInTheHouse2, 2022).

Conclusion

The nature of impending fatherhood is that you are doing something that you're unqualified to do, and then you become qualified while doing it. –John Green

As a first-time dad, your pregnancy experience will never be the same as the expectant mother, but you have a vital role in providing emotional and physical support to your partner throughout the different stages of pregnancy. Each week of the nine months of the pregnancy has its own challenges, joyous moments, pregnancy symptoms, anxieties, stress, and pure happiness. It is a whirlwind of a journey, but at the end of it all, it will be glorious when you hold your baby in your loving arms. It is helpful to know what you can expect week by week during the stages of pregnancy and get tips to help you along the way. You and the mother of your unborn child must have a healthy parenting relationship that has a firm foundation built on communication, trust, and devotion to your child. There are many ways to cultivate a healthy parenting relationship with your partner, such as establishing clear boundaries, constructing a regular schedule, being willing to be flexible, deferring to each other, and sometimes agreeing to disagree and compromise on important matters about your child together. When you have reached common ground with the mother of your unborn child, think about some fun, creative ways to bond with your baby while they are in your partner's pregnant belly. Some of the ideas shared in this book were creating sonogram art, imagining the world of adventure you will have with them, singing your favorite songs, and reading children's books to them. You could continue doing these fun things with them once they are born. Bonding with your child is one of the most rewarding and exciting ways of becoming the parent you always dreamt of becoming one day.

Before that happens, there is the delivery of your baby that needs to occur first. Constructing a birth plan can help ensure your expectations and desires for your childbirth are known by the doctor, nurses, and other medical staff. You can get templates of birth plans online, or when you enroll in birthing classes, you can get a birth plan that suits your preferable birthing method, which is a great benefit. Once you have come up with your preferred birth plan, immediately schedule an appointment with your partner's doctor to discuss it with them, and advocate for your care regarding issues, such as augmentation of labor and pain medication during childbirth. Ensure you leave no rock unturned when you have this discussion with your doctor, and your views are crucial in having a well-thought-out birth plan. Also, on the other hand, prepare for the unexpected. Remember Mo Mulla's story? So, consider learning everything you can about delivering a baby to prepare for the possibility of needing to deliver your baby at home in case the paramedics arrive late or your partner gets into active labor while at home. While you are at it, there are many lists of essential items shared in this book that will prepare you for your baby's arrival and ultimately make the transition into parenthood a lot easier. Hopefully, you have gained helpful information in this book and have a great time applying what you have learned in this book!

References

Alio, A. P., Lewis, C. A., Scarborough, K., Harris, K., & Fiscella, K. (2013). A community perspective on the role of fathers during pregnancy: A qualitative study. *BioMedical Central Pregnancy and Childbirth,* *13*(60), 1 - 11. https://doi.org/10.1186/1471-2393-13-60

Brown, A., & Davies, R. (2014). Fathers' experiences of supporting breastfeeding: Challenges for breastfeeding promotion and education. *Maternal & Child Nutrition,* *10*(4), 510 - 526. doi: 10.1111/mcn.12129

Cecil, J. (October 07, 2019). My susccess in co-parenting. *Medium.* Retrieved from https://anewpathdsm.medium.com/my-success-in-co-parenting-ccde9cab8cd4

Centers for Disease Control and Prevention. (January 31, 2022). Substancce abuse during pregnancy. *Centers for Disease Control and Prevention.* Retrieved from https://www.cdc.gov/reproductivehealth/maternalinfanthealth/substance-abuse/substance-abuse-during-pregnancy.htm

Clarke, E. (2022). Healthy snacks to keep on hand. *Well plated.* Retrieved from https://www.wellplated.com/5-healthy-snacks/

Coleman, P. A. (May 05, 2020). What expectant parents should include and consider. *Fatherly.* Retrieved from https://www.fatherly.com/health-science/build-birth-plan-pregnancy-expecting

Family Action. (2022). Basil's story: Birth and pregnancy from a dad's experience. *Family Action.* Retrieved from https://www.family-action.org.uk/our-voices/2020/06/19/basils-story-birth-and-pregnancy-from-a-dads-perspective/

Gordon, K. (September 08, 2013). Eight ways dad-to-be can bond with baby now. *Parents.* Retrieved from https://www.parents.com/parenting/dads/101/ways-dad-to-be-can-bond-with-baby-now/

KidsInTheHouse2. (January 04, 2022). How to properly prepare for baby's arrival as a first-time dad? *Kids in the house.* Retrieved from https://www.kidsinthehouse.com/blogs/kidsinthehouse2/how-to-properly-prepare-for-babys-arrival-as-a-first-time-dad

Ledenfors, A., & Berterö, C. (2016). First-time fathers' experiences of normal childbirth. *Midwifery, 40,*

26-31.
https://doi.org/10.1016/j.midw.2016.05.013

Mayo Clinic. (March 12, 2021). Pregnancy week by week. *Mayo Clinic.* Retrieved from https://www.mayoclinic.org/healthy-lifestyle/pregnancy-week-by-week/in-depth/pregnancy-and-exercise/art-20046896

Mulla, M. (2022). A father's unique story on delivering his own daughter! (At home, unplanned). *Henpicked.* Retrieved from https://henpicked.net/a-fathers-unique-story-on-delivering-his-own-daughter-at-home-unplanned/

Nadeau, A. (October 03, 2019). 75 Heartwarming quotes about dads and being a father. *The Dad.* Retrieved from https://www.thedad.com/75-heartwarming-quotes-about-fatherhood/

Oberg, E. (2022). 7 Childbirth delivery methods and types. *Medicine Net.* Retrieved from https://www.medicinenet.com/7_childbirth_an d_delivery_methods/article.htm

Pampers. (December 13, 2021). Newborn baby checklist - the must-haves and more. *Pampers.* Retrieved from https://www.pampers.com/en-us/pregnancy/preparing-for-your-new-baby/article/newborn-baby-checklist\

Rodgers, L. (July 9, 2020). Week by week pregnancy advice for expecting dads and partners. *What To Expect.* Retrieved from https://www.whattoexpect.com/pregnancy/for-dad/week-by-week-pregnancy-advice-dads-partners/

Team Peanut. (2022). 50 Amazing pregnancy quotes to remember. *Peanut.* Retrieved from https://www.peanut-app.io/blog/pregnancy-quotes

Toub, M. (June 08, 2021). The science of how fatherhood transforms you. *Today's Parent.* Retrieved from https://www.todaysparent.com/family/parenting/the-science-of-how-fatherhood-transforms-you/

Villines, Z. (January 16, 2019). Couvade syndrome: When expectant dads get pregnancy symptoms. *Good Therapy.* Retrieved from https://www.goodtherapy.org/blog/couvade-syndrome-when-expectant-dads-get-pregnancy-symptoms-0116197

Wolf, J. (October 05, 2020). 10 Signs of a healthy, effective co-parenting relationship. *Very Well Family.* Retrieved from https://www.verywellfamily.com/signs-of-a-healthy-coparenting-relationship-2997282#citation-5

Woolfall, K., Frith, L., Gamble, C., Gilbert, R., Mok, Q., & Young, B. (2015). How parents and practitioners experience research without prior consent (deferred consent) for emergency research involving children with life threatening conditions: A mixed method study. *British Medical Journal Apen, 5*(9), http://dx.doi.org/10.1136/bmjopen-2015- 008522.

Printed in Dunstable, United Kingdom